90 Days, 90 Ways

90 Days, 90 Ways

A Book of Daily Meditations
by Recovering Nicotine Addicts

Nicotine Anonymous World Services

Copyright © 2004 by Nicotine Anonymous

All rights reserved. No part of this publication may be reproduced, stored in a retrieval system, or transmitted, in any form or by any means, electronic, mechanical, photocopying, recording, or otherwise, without the prior written permission of

Nicotine Anonymous World Services
6333 Mockingbird Lane, Suite 147–817
Dallas, Texas 75214

Published by Nicotine Anonymous World Services,
a nonprofit tax-exempt corporation.

Nicotine Anonymous website address:
www.nicotine-anonymous.org

Manufactured in Canada and printed on acid-free paper.

FIRST EDITION 2004

2 3 4 5 6 7 8 9 10 / 16 15 14 13

DAY ONE

Bob's Eleventh Step Prayer

God, direct my thinking in this upcoming day. Humble me and guide me.
Show me the way. Keep dishonest and self-seeking motives away, and do not allow self-pity to enter my day.
Keep selfish motives out of all my thoughts, and remind me often of what you have taught.
When I am faced with some indecision today, show me the right course and guide the way.
Give me intuitive thoughts as you inspire me, or give me a decision so my mind can be free.
Teach me how to relax and take it easy too. I know the right answers will come from you.
Don't let me struggle if the going gets rough. Your same right answers will still be enough.
Place my thinking more on an inspired plane. Let me come to rely on it and avoid the pain.
Above all, God, give me freedom from self-will. Guide each step while I'm climbing the hill.
Remind me to ask for right action or thought when I'm agitated, in doubt or even distraught.
Thy will be done. I'm no longer running the show.
I love You, God, and I just wanted You to know.

DAY TWO

Every day we wake up, we have choices to make up.
—NICOTINE ANONYMOUS MEMBER

Each day we can begin by deciding our behavior regarding such things as hygiene, exercise, and food. We can choose to pray for guidance and support for this day. These choices will also affect our choice of attitude with which we begin our day. We can create a plan with these choices, and then take active steps to carry it out as well as we can at each moment. We seek progress, not perfection. We humbly practice the intentions of our own choices.

As nicotine addicts, once we choose to use our drug of choice, we begin to lose our gift of choice. "Using" controls our behavior and our attitudes. "Using" controls with whom we associate with, the places we go, and the situations we end up in. "Using" causes us to lose choices all along the way and thus we become lost. Eventually we may get sick, institutionalized, or die as a direct result of our addiction.

Choosing a path of recovery, rather than the closed cycle of addiction, improves our lives. Recovery opens us to new possibilities "beyond our wildest dreams" or in ways that we have previously been too sick to see.

Today, I am aware of my power to make new choices, create new behaviors, and enjoy new attitudes that improve the quality of my life.

DAY THREE

No one can make you feel inferior without your consent.
—ELEANOR ROOSEVELT

What can be more demeaning than being a "dumpster smoker"? You know what I mean. I'd leave my job to go outside and smoke; or, leave the theatre, or the restaurant, or my own home. I felt so humiliated. I knew I needed that smoke no matter the cost, time or place. No matter who was hurt, or offended, or annoyed, nicotine was my be-all and end-all. I could not live with it, and I could not live without it.

No wonder I had no self-worth. I was caught, trapped, snared, and hopeless. Finally, I was desperate enough to go to a Nicotine Anonymous meeting. I was fearful. Would they accept someone who was still smoking? Or throw me out?

Thank you, Higher Power, for giving me a place to grow with other nicotine addicts who understand. Thank for the tools of the program, meetings, slogans, sponsorship, and, especially, prayer. By Your grace, I am free for today and becoming more whole and complete each day.

Today, I choose to use the tools of the program to continue growing.

DAY FOUR

We cannot change anything unless we accept it. Condemnation does not liberate, it oppresses.
  —C. G. JUNG

All the curses I can utter, all the self loathing I can swallow, will not bring about long lasting change. These patterns of behavior only reinforce the negative cycle of addiction. I used nicotine to numb my negative feelings. Condemnation just triggers me into my addiction.

Step One asks me to accept and admit that I am a powerless addict and that my life is suffering from the continual abuse of nicotine. Until I accept the truth of my circumstances I am merely pretending, rather than tending to my life. Only as I move toward the complete acceptance of myself can I be truly open for the healing I receive from my Higher Power.

Until then, I repeat the same old excuses and defects over and over again while expecting different results. This insanity always takes me to the same place. I put nicotine into my body for relief, but then I feel condemned and demoralized afterwards.

With acceptance I can stop running away. The trigger to condemn myself is defused. In recovery I surrender to the truth and the help that can set me free.

Today, I accept the truth. My surrender eases the harshness and opens me to real change.

DAY FIVE

The pursuit of perfection often impedes progress.
—GEORGE WILL

I get busy. I push. I talk a lot. I spend an exorbitant amount of time on the computer or the telephone. I forget to eat or I eat too much. I sleep a lot or not enough. I get short fused and aggressive or meek and passive. I don't exercise. I consume excess sugar and caffeine.

I get into this duality, this high-low, black-white, meek or wild state of mind. I forget that I just quit using nicotine and that my body and mind is detoxifying from all the chemicals and poisons that I ingested daily on an hourly basis.

When I am reminded that I recently quit by my sponsor, my Nicotine Anonymous group or my friends, I remember to lighten up and relax. I remember the slogan "Let Go and Let God" and again allow my Higher Power to take care of the details and me. I start back at the first three steps. I am powerless. There is a power greater than myself and I made a decision to turn my will and my life over to my Higher Power.

Today, I may start acting compulsively, but I am open to reminders to "Let Go and Let God."

DAY SIX

We took a realistic look at the power nicotine had over us, and we saw that its control was absolute.
NICOTINE ANONYMOUS, THE BOOK

I smoked from infancy, inhaling second hand smoke from both of my parents who were heavy smokers. I became addicted first hand when I was 16. I believed I could beat the odds and be a recreational, controlled smoker. Tobacco beat me every day. After thirty years of being a heavy smoker, and countless attempts at stopping, I found myself at Nicotine Anonymous meetings, continuing to smoke for months.

Then the miracle happened. I have not had tobacco or nicotine in any form for over four years.

I still attend meetings. I am so grateful to live nicotine free one day at a time. I believe praying for the willingness to quit, and doing the God work with my Higher Power's guidance through our fellowship makes it possible for me to live nicotine free.

Today I thank God and the fellowship I found in Nicotine Anonymous and for the miracle of living free.

DAY SEVEN

Nowhere can man find a quieter or more untroubled retreat than in his own soul.
—MARCUS AURELIUS

Earlier in my life, I never thought of asking God to relieve me of my obsession to use nicotine. It seemed very normal because so many people I knew used nicotine in some form. Somewhere it quit seeming normal; people I knew were quitting.

Eventually I could not deny the dangers. The diseases caused by my drug of choice are killers. I began to realize that I had to quit.

I found Nicotine Anonymous and the Twelve Steps. Prayer and meditation bring me closer to my Higher Power, and help me on my path to recovery.

Today, I thank God for helping me live nicotine free one day at a time, for the rest of my life.

DAY EIGHT

The space for what you want in your life is already filled by what you settled for instead.
—GRACE TERRY

For twenty years I struggled to quit smoking, but I never could stay quit. Fourteen of those years were after part of my left lung was removed. Every time I quit it was progressively harder, physically and emotionally. Every time I quit, I did so for a shorter period. I did not believe I had another quit in me. And, I knew that if I tried again and failed again, I would die smoking. I was hopelessly addicted, and the addiction was gaining power.

Then my teenage son got involved with alcohol and drugs. Early in his treatment, he confronted me. He said that all his life, every morning, he would listen to my hacking. He had always been afraid I would die, and he would have no one. How could I have been so blind to the damage I had been doing to my beloved, only child?

I found Nicotine Anonymous. You showed me the lies about nicotine. You were happy to live without nicotine. I learned to stop for a moment of truth every time I saw someone else smoking. Rather than being jealous because, "they can smoke and I can't," I learned to, "thank God I am free today." In a remarkably short time those words became a true expression, instead of a wish.

Today, I am grateful to be alive, happy, and healthy. I love life and life is great.

DAY NINE

Admitted we were powerless over nicotine, that our lives had become unmanageable.
—STEP ONE

I tried to stop using nicotine every day for at least twenty years. It never occurred to me that I was addicted to nicotine. It never occurred to me that I was powerless over something. I had a million and one excuses about why I was still puffing away: My life was too stressful, someone upset me, I had a test, a deadline, a cold, etc. It was quite amazing the number of different problems that kept me from quitting. It seemed much more acceptable to me to have a reason why it was impossible to quit right now than to think I had absolutely no control over my stopping.

My friends and colleagues listened to my many schemes to defeat nicotine. After a week or two they would see me using as much as usual. After a while, I grew too embarrassed to tell people that I was quitting.

When I first came to Nicotine Anonymous I was just going through the motions of the latest scheme that I had discovered. At some point I thought that I could just go to the meetings and hope that whatever knowledge the group had would seep into my brain. I was powerless and at last I understood the first step.

Today, I understand I had been participating in a grand hoax; I haven't given up anything at all.

DAY TEN

A Puff Away From a Pack a Day
—Nicotine Anonymous Member

I like to remember that my addiction is ever present, that I am only a "puff away from a pack a day." It keeps me humble, and helps me remember how powerless I am over this addiction.

Today, Higher Power, help me to remember that I am powerless over nicotine and that with your help I will be thankful for each day without nicotine.

DAY ELEVEN

The most powerful agent of growth and transformation is something much more basic than any technique: a change of heart.
—JOHN WELWOOD

Those horrible "afters." I am constantly reminded of all the times I smoked: after using the phone, after a meal, after sex. What do I do now?

I have to remember that abstinence is a minute-by-minute, hour-by-hour, and day-by-day experience, one day at a time. Also I recall that the craving will pass whether I smoke or not. A craving is simply my body telling me it is time to put a call in to my Higher Power.

Today I will call on my Higher Power to stay with me and support me when I want to smoke.

DAY TWELVE

Admitted I am powerless over nicotine, that my life had become unmanageable.
—STEP ONE, NICOTINE ANONYMOUS

In June 1978 I was trying, again, to quit using nicotine. That time I was using an aid, a type of filter system. A friend was quitting with me, so I had some support.

On the 30th of that month, I was down to the fourth filter. That day I wound up at the hospital because I could not breathe and was in severe pain. My doctor said I had pneumonia in my right lung, and my left lung was partially collapsed. I had to be hospitalized, and could not even go home to pack a bag. He sent me to have some lunch while I waited for the thoracic surgeon to be available to see me.

First I had a cigarette with a filter. Then I decided I needed more nicotine so I covered the hole in the filter. Then I pulled off the filter and just smoked. In that hour, I chain smoked most of a pack. I was gasping for breath. I was turning blue from lack of oxygen. Still the most important thing to me was feeding my addiction.

I did not get to Nicotine Anonymous for another fourteen years. For all those years, I believed that nicotine was the only thing that made my life possible. I knew I was addicted, that was why I had not quit. Until I got to Nicotine Anonymous, I had not admitted my life was unmanageable. Step One has two parts, and both are vitally important to my recovery.

Today, every time I see another nicotine addict, I take time to thank God I am happy, joyous and free.

DAY THIRTEEN

Some people change when they see the light, others when they feel the heat.
—CAROLINE SCHOEDER

When I found Nicotine Anonymous, I was taking care of my Mother who was dying from emphysema. I was also suffering from emphysema in earlier stages. I came to meetings for months, but still struggled to quit. I got a sponsor, then I got a second sponsor, and still I struggled.

Finally one day, I was at the emergency room because my bronchitis was so bad I could not breathe. While I waited, I wrote in my journal. I wrote that nicotine was my only connection to normalcy, to health, to sociability. For the first time, I realized how much power I had given to nicotine, and just how insane I had become.

I continued to give in and smoke. I still thought that just the next cigarette was not so bad. Eventually I was ready to face reality. I was ready to accept cravings, knowing they are feelings, not facts, and that they would pass if I just did not continue to feed my addiction.

Today I thank God for the fellowship of Nicotine Anonymous, all those members who loved and accepted me through my struggle to recovery.

DAY FOURTEEN

When your world is shaking and you are praying that the world will stop shaking, consider that maybe your Higher Power is doing the shaking.
—NICOTINE ANONYMOUS MEMBER

In my smoking days, I would get bronchitis at least once every winter, and when it got bad enough I would go to the doctor for antibiotics. At the clinic, there would always be a different doctor who would give me a lecture that went something like this:

"Your smoking is causing bronchitis and I can see by your chart that you get it at least once every year. I encourage you to stop smoking before you do more serious damage to your health."

I would walk out of the clinic, angry because a young doctor had lectured me again, and telling myself that of course smoking was not causing my bronchitis. I would light up a cigarette and cough some more. But I can tell you today that I have not had bronchitis once in the years since I quit smoking.

Today, I pray that when my Higher Power shows me a truth I can hear it and believe it.

DAY FIFTEEN

We relax and take it easy. We don't struggle.
—ALCOHOLICS ANONYMOUS, *BIG BOOK*

I love the slogan "Easy Does It." It seems to be my nature to stress over life's everyday events. In the past, I thought chewing tobacco reduced my stress. Now I know nicotine addiction added to my stress levels, and pulled down my self-esteem and feelings of security.

I have also learned that sometimes I can't help getting stressed. I feel my blood pressure rising as well as other stress-related symptoms, and want some relief. Often just repeating "easy does it" gives me the feeling if some relief. I choose to remember that nothing is worth smoking over. Nothing. I remember that to go back to chewing over a stressful situation would become a permanent answer to a temporary problem.

Today, in any stressful situation, instead of reaching for nicotine, I will breathe deeply, think a relaxing thought. Easy Does It.

DAY SIXTEEN

We became willing to give up the notion of controlling the use of nicotine.
—NICOTINE ANONYMOUS

I learned the hard way about becoming a nicotine addict. I thought it was other people who got hooked, not me. I thought I could take it or leave it. But I always wanted more and soon craved nicotine when I did not smoke. When I tried to quit, I did not like the feelings that I later learned were the result of withdrawal.

Sometimes I would make it nicotine-free a couple of weeks. Then I'd break down and have just one. After that first cigarette, my addiction was activated and I was powerless. I was back to craving cigarettes by the carton. My willpower was gone.

Finally I learned that it was the first one that hooked me. It is not the second or third or hundredth hit that does the damage. It is the first one; that first hit. Through the process of becoming willing, I have learned that no matter how compelling the thought of just one jolt of nicotine, the urge will pass and I will be free of nicotine one day at a time.

Today, I remember that I have chosen to live free of the hideous nicotine addiction. It is the right choice for me.

DAY SEVENTEEN

Many people have found strength far beyond their own by relying on a power greater than themselves.
— ALCOHOLICS ANONYMOUS

Before coming to Nicotine Anonymous, I had tried on my own to quit smoking for twenty-five years. I guess I had to admit one hundred percent that without help, quitting was too much for me. Then I could ask for help from others who had struggled as I had and who have been able to live nicotine free.

With the experience, strength and hope shared from the group, I started to try again to quit. Still I did not have enough power. When I put out my last cigarette I knew that my faith in the power of my God would be the power I needed.

In the process of quitting I gave up many times each day. But each morning and each craving I asked my God to help me not to smoke no matter what. The help came when I surrendered and God answered my prayer by doing for me what I could not do for myself.

Without the love and support of Nicotine Anonymous and my Higher Power, quitting using nicotine and living life is too much for me.

Today, I am grateful for the love and support of Nicotine Anonymous and my Higher Power, as I accept all that life presents to me.

DAY EIGHTEEN

Often the search proves more profitable than the goal.
—E. L. KONIGSBURG

My Higher Power is always available to me. When I am angry or frustrated, I can take the time to notice that I cannot change the situation or person on which I am focusing anger. Then I can "let go and let God" take care of it. I do not have the energy to fix everything. I want to be free to enjoy the wonders of life.

I can let my Higher Power decide how things will turn out. I can let myself be soft, open to God's will and be gentle with myself. I can relax into God's loving care.

If I want relief about something today, I can let God help me. I can remember that I am powerless over nicotine and ask for my Higher Power's guidance, comfort and wisdom.

Today, I will open my clenched hands to receive God's love and help.

DAY NINETEEN

What will I do today? It may depend upon which "will" I chose to listen to.
—NICOTINE ANONYMOUS MEMBER

Human beings have what we call "free will." This may be true, but the people, places, and things in our surroundings also influence our thinking. We say we have "willpower," but even "normal people" find themselves admitting, "I knew I shouldn't have done that, but . . ."

As addicts our willpower has not been sufficient to help us stop using drugs. After all, our will has been conditioned with the determined thinking of: I want nicotine, my drug of choice; I will have nicotine, my drug of choice.

Coming "to believe that a power greater than ourselves can restore us to sanity" can mean becoming open-minded to consider the guidance and wisdom of a counselor and/or a sponsor, the group, the program, and a belief in a Higher Power of our own understanding.

Today, as I open myself to the possibility of being restored, I do not lose my will; I gain a greater Will to help recover my life.

DAY TWENTY

We are not cured. . . . What we really have is a daily reprieve contingent on the maintenance of our spiritual condition.
—BILL W.

I never believed I could stop using nicotine. I made a few, pitiful attempts over the years, but I could not do it by myself. What was the problem? Was I so very weak or so very stubborn? Was it a lack of willpower? Or too much self-will? It did not matter. I was hopelessly stuck, afraid and imprisoned by nicotine.

I prayed for my Higher Power to help me. I read Alcoholics Anonymous', "Came to Believe," a book about how the obsession to use alcohol was removed from people by their Higher Power. I could not do this under my own power. Nicotine's control of me was absolute. And then, one morning, my nicotine obsession was lifted.

What a gift! To be free of this nightmare was a miracle. Part one was receiving the gift: part two is my maintaining this freedom by constant vigilance. I know where my freedom comes from. I thank my Higher Power and talk to Him each day; aim for a gratitude attitude; attend meetings; read Twelve Step literature, and share my experience, strength and hope with others. Life is so good without addiction, and I am willing to work every day to stay free.

Today, by the Grace of my Higher Power, I am free of nicotine. Please help me to stay that way.

DAY TWENTY-ONE

Live today as if there were no tomorrow and the present is yours forever.
—JEAN MANTHEI

Some of the tools I have discovered are: my Higher Power, meditation, staying with the urge and riding it out, accepting discomfort, and the "five D's"—deep breath, distract, delay, do something else, and drink water. I do what works for me, not what I think I should or must do. I have found that the biggest reasons I relapsed was that I did not use my own coping strategies, including prayer.

Finding the peace that knows no understanding comes with acceptance and love of others and me. The gains of recovery far outweigh the costs and pain of using nicotine and relapsing. I focus on the fact that, yes, there will be moments of discomfort, but also that there will be more laughter, love, affection, creativity, joy, increased control, greater self-esteem, and other feelings of all kinds. Are these not more desirable that the self-abuse suffered from the choice to use nicotine, and the resulting sense of despair and hopelessness?

Today, I will continue my recovery by accepting discomfort and opening myself to a greater goodness.

DAY TWENTY-TWO

Only those who can see the invisible can do the impossible.
—Albert Einstein

When I am feeling the stress or pressure that used to drive me to nicotine, I remember that I have the power to choose a new response today.

I choose not to simply follow, and fall prey to, my initial emotional reaction to any outside stimulus or agitation. I ask myself whether I can control or change the situation or stressor. I choose to put things in the hands of my Higher Power, and I consider my part in making things better. No matter what may be happening outside of me, no matter what people may do and say, no one has the power to make me feel any particular emotion or feeling. No one can take away my freedom to step back and choose my response.

I see and hear people who react to every little stimulus and agitation. They seem to take it all upon themselves like bricks on their backs, weighing themselves down until they cannot stand it any longer, and must either find escape or collapse.

Today, I have the power to live differently. Through our fellowship and with the strength of my Higher Power, I choose to live serenely and without the need of escape.

DAY TWENTY-THREE

Sometimes in the winds of change we find our true direction.
—MAC ANDERSON

I see my Higher Power as the very replacement over the kingship that nicotine had in my life. After endless attempts to quit using by my own power and good deeds, being Mr. Fellowship, starting meetings, people pleasing, and caring what others think, I only fell flat on my face by slipping again and again.

There came that day when I realized that all of my resources had failed me. But, thank God, recovering members of our program were inspired to write a book. Page twelve states, "a return to nicotine was part of the process of hitting a real bottom."

Now, it doesn't tell me to go and feed my addiction, but it does say I will learn more about my condition. Through the failures, I learned that, left to my own power, I am destined to live in my addiction to the bitter end. My Higher Power, my only defense to this deadly disease, has now taken the throne. All I do is serve the Good King, take correction and direction, and give what I can to my fellow sufferers.

Today, I realize that I have no effective mental defense against this disease. My King has done for me what I could not do for myself.

DAY TWENTY-FOUR

If you have the courage to begin, you have the courage to succeed.
—DAVID VISCOTT

The last time I used nicotine, I had already gone nearly sixty days without feeding my addiction. Then came a craving. I sat at my kitchen table telling it to go away, and it said no. I knelt down and prayed, it still it said no. I went to a meeting, but still it said no. I called at least seven other nicotine addicts, but the craving continued to say, "no way." I did everything humanly possible to be rid of that relentless craving. Nothing worked. My addiction won.

However, I learned a valuable lesson. I realized I was still trying to control my addiction. I realized my best efforts left me with no defense from my addiction. I needed one hundred percent Divine help to stop. I finally and fully conceded my powerlessness over nicotine, and started letting God provide my defense.

I am now working Step Eight and Step Nine with my sponsor. I am allowing God and my sponsor to guide me to freedom from nicotine. If not for Nicotine Anonymous, I would still be a slave, worshipping nicotine as King.

Today, I remember to surrender my addiction to God, and I thank God for keeping me on the path of joy and serenity.

DAY TWENTY-FIVE

Take God out of the church and give Him a home. He will thank you and He will share His toys!
—LON SPIEGELMAN

The larger the grain of sand, the easier it is to handle. It is life's tiniest grains that seem to slip out of our control.

The only procrastination program that works in a positive manner is the one I used in relation to my nicotine addiction.

It is the Positive Procrastination Program, or PPP. When I get that craving for a cigarette, I utter the letters PPP and put off lighting up for a set period of time, usually a few minutes.

As I distance myself in time from the initial craving, maybe two or three minutes of time, I forget about lighting up until the next craving. As I continued to recover, I put several PPPs together until finally I was able to quit nicotine completely.

Today, I will make time to pause and remember I can choose serentiy.

DAY TWENTY-SIX

I realize I had been living a grand hoax. I haven't given up anything at all.
—PROMISES OF NICOTINE ANONYMOUS

Nicotine limited me. I was enslaved. When I started smoking it was to be a part of, to join my peers. After thirty-five years as a practicing addict, I was no longer accepted. My peers had quit. I felt like an outcast.

I lived in fear that I would be forced to be somewhere I could not smoke. Long plane flights were no longer possible.

I have been free of the compulsion to plan my life around my nicotine addiction for five years. I am free to go anywhere I want, and to stay as long as I want. I am free.

Today God, I choose the gift of living free of nicotine. God, don't let me forget the restrictions nicotine demanded in my life.

DAY TWENTY-SEVEN

"We knew we would have to quit the deadly business of living alone with our conflicts, and in honesty confide these to God and to another human being."
—ALCOHOLICS ANONYMOUS

I was having trouble sleeping; I just generally did not feel well. I had been calling my sponsor every day for over five months, but I was reluctant to let him know how I was really feeling. My sponsor had the tendency to ask me to read the literature when I was not doing well, and I did not want to bother with that.

Finally I leveled with my sponsor, who pointed out I was trying to bargain with God. I was saying, "God, if you just let me have my way on this one thing, I will continue to surrender to Your will for me." I was refusing to surrender, and my sponsor told me I sounded quite miserable. He was right. I was miserable, but wanted desperately to be happy, joyous and free. Instead of giving me the answers again, my sponsor said the answer was in the book if I wanted to read it.

I was reminded I need to pray only for God's will, not mine, and continue to pray throughout the day whenever I find myself insisting on my way. I found relief.

Today, I thank God for my sponsor and all those who hold up a mirror so I can see myself as I truly am.

DAY TWENTY-EIGHT

When I am stuck in traffic, miss an elevator, turn back to answer a ringing telephone ... all the little things that annoy me.... I think to myself, this is exactly where God wants me to be at this very moment.
—UNKNOWN

I was possessed by a demon of indescribable power, a demon that seems oblivious to my will, a demon that robbed my sense of self worth. I could list dozens of reasons, but really needed no provocation to continue to pamper my addiction. I could set no boundaries for my need to smoke. Why else would I light another when I had one burning?

I found relief through surrender. Divine intervention coupled with my sincere desire to quit, provided the dynamic strength to break free from this demon.

There were many obstacles on my path to ultimate cessation. My un-medicated anger made me a menace to those around me and to myself. But my desire to quit and stay quit was stronger than the anguish over my inability to control my emotions.

I am nicotine free. Recovery allows me to make amends for my aggressive and self-absorbed behavior. Living nicotine free is itself a living amends.

Today, I thank God I have the ability to deal with life's inevitable conflicts, without using nicotine.

DAY TWENTY-NINE

I came to meetings for three years and still couldn't stop, until I finally realized it was true, I couldn't stop.
—NICOTINE ANONYMOUS, THE BOOK

I was coughing so hard I was afraid I was going to pass out. I did not want to eat because I always went into a coughing fit afterwards. I was sleeping in my chair instead of in my bed because I could not breathe lying down. I cleared my throat constantly. I had bronchitis twice in the past three months. I had lost so much weight I could see the veins in my stomach. I knew I had to quit, but how many times had I said that before but kept on smoking?

Then it dawned on me. I really was powerless so God was going to have to do it, or it would not get done. Instead of fighting the compulsion, my part became giving it to God. I turned it over every time the urge came. They said God could and would if He were sought. They were right. I cannot remember the last time I had the urge to smoke, and it has been eight months.

Today, I thank God for doing for me what I cannot do myself.

DAY THIRTY

The only requirement for Nicotine Anonymous membership is a desire to stop using nicotine.
—TRADITION THREE

When I first came to Nicotine Anonymous, I was still smoking. I quit then because I was worried about what the group thought of me. That was not a strong enough reason for me to continue to not smoke, because after twenty-nine days, I started smoking again, and I stopped coming to meetings.

A year later, I returned. This time I was determined to surrender my addiction to God. It took me another fifteen months to learn how to let go. Tradition Three gave me permission to keep coming back to meetings so I could learn.

I did eventually learn to trust my Higher Power. I set my quit date. With God's help I became willing to endure, even to embrace, the cravings.

I kept coming back because I had to, and because Nicotine Anonymous said I could.

Today, I remember the words of Mother Teresa, "God does not call us to be successful. He calls us to be faithful."

DAY THIRTY-ONE

I am indeed a practical dreamer.... I want to convert my dreams into realities as far as possible.
—MOHANDAS GANDHI

I used to be enslaved by nicotine. That may sound like an exaggeration, but nicotine prevented me from knowing myself and doing what I really wanted to do in life. I was an addict. I smoked one to two packs a day for forty years.

I never felt I could rely on my own abilities. I needed something to alter my mood. I thought I could think better, write better, drive better, and talk more intelligently when I smoked.

The last twenty years of my addiction was spent in fear of the consequences, but also in fear of life without cigarettes. I was trapped.

Today, thanks to the Twelve Steps of Nicotine Anonymous and my group, I am a different person. I am free. I am free to pursue a life I could only dream about before.

Recently, I celebrated my sixth nicotine-free anniversary in a village in South Africa, helping teach English, science and math, and working on community development projects as a Peace Corps volunteer.

Today, I love what I am doing, and I love being nicotine free.

DAY THIRTY-TWO

There is nothing permanent except change.
—HERACLITES

I do not like change. As a Nicotine addict, change can be completely devastating for me. When change comes into my life, whether I have invited it in or it is knocking down the door uninvited, I lose the sense of control that seems essential to my being. I feel best when I'm in control and change embodies a total lack of control.

During times of change I need to remember the Serenity Prayer—"God, grant me the serenity to accept the things I cannot change...." I don't really have any power over the direction my life goes, even when I believe I am in control. But no matter what path my life takes, my Higher Power is always there to hold my hand and to guide me.

"Living Life on Life's Terms" is a good philosophy to practice. It is an acceptance of whatever turns my life seems to make. When I accept it rather than fight it, I find I enjoy my path so much more and serenity really can find a place in my heart. Fortunately for me, change—both good and bad—is part of the journey of recovery. Whatever shape it takes, it molds me into the new person I am becoming.

Thank you, God, for giving me the courage to change with serenity.

DAY THIRTY-THREE

Today is the beginning of a wonderful day until someone comes and messes it up....
—UNKNOWN

I discovered this truthful saying during lent on a piece of china and it really made me think. It does not always have to be someone else but can actually be me who ruins the day. I am the king of self-deception, and not only that, but I also believe my own tricks which are tangled up with problems that I wrote, directed, produced and starred in. In the end I blame everyone else except myself, thus falling in the trap of "poor lil' ole me."

At moments like that, I can remember the Serenity Prayer and put myself in His Hands (Step Three). "The Boss" (my God) is the only one who really knows what will happen, and I am only a small instrument of His will, trying to achieve—although I do not always succeed—day by day.

Today, I will pause and look at what I am doing to create discomfort.

DAY THIRTY-FOUR

As long as I am working on quitting smoking, my Higher Power will take care of everything else.
—NICOTINE ANONYMOUS MEMBER

In the beginning, just staying off nicotine is hard enough. So I have to let my Higher Power handle whatever else comes along. As the days pass and my emotions settle down and the cravings lessen, then I can think about what else I need to be doing, like working the steps, and deepening my contact with my Higher Power.

Today, Higher Power, thanks for watching over my life and supporting me in my desire to overcome nicotine.

DAY THIRTY-FIVE

The wind of God's grace is always blowing, but you must raise your sails.
—VIVEKANANDA

After almost thirty years of smoking cigarettes, I finally realized I was insane. This enlightenment came to me one morning at 6:00 AM, as I lit my first smoke of the day. I had been awakened at 4:00 AM, once again; coughing so hard I could barely catch my breath. And here I was, two hours later, smoking a cigarette. Insanity!

Divine guidance led me to a counselor. I told him how I had come to the realization that I was insane, and in reply he handed me a copy of *Nicotine Anonymous The Book*. I realized that I was being asked to walk the walk, instead of just talking the talk. I admitted that I was an addict to nicotine, I was powerless over my addiction, and that my life had become unmanageable.

I have not used nicotine since December 22, 2000. People congratulated me and praised me for my willpower. My willpower was not strong enough; my willpower had been losing the battle with my addiction for years. Only when I surrendered my will to my Higher Power was I graced with freedom from the chains of my addiction.

Today, I am willing to listen to my Higher Power, and to act as I am guided.

DAY THIRTY-SIX

There are two ways to live your life—one is as though nothing is a miracle, the other is as though everything is a miracle.
—ALBERT EINSTEIN

As a nicotine user I thought that the only way I would be able to stop living in my addiction would be by Divine intervention. I thought that some day the craving to use nicotine would be lifted and I would easily stop.

Upon entering Nicotine Anonymous, one of my early thoughts was that Divine intervention did not do it, but that Nicotine Anonymous did, and that I could accept the craving and not act on it.

After a little more time free from nicotine, I realized that it was a Higher Power that led me to Nicotine Anonymous, and that I had to let go and let God run my life.

Today, I acknowledge God's presence in my life, and I am grateful to surrender my will and my life.

DAY THIRTY-SEVEN

Came to believe that a Power greater than ourselves could restore us to sanity.
—STEP TWO

Feeling grateful that I am an ex-smoker for some years now keeps me going when I wake up from a smoking dream or see someone puffing away on a nice summer day. One tool I use is to say, "God, I pray for the person smoking," each time I notice someone smoking. It helps me not feel deprived.

I always need to remember that I gratefully *chose* not to smoke; no one is depriving me. Smoking is my enemy, never my friend. Nicotine use is always the problem, never the solution. Health is so precious and not smoking is good for my health.

Not smoking is a miracle for an addict like me, and I thank my Higher Power for this gift. Though I avoid nicotine use these days, I feel tremendous compassion for the nicotine addict who still suffers, and recovering addicts who still get the urge.

Today, I gratefully choose freedom from addiction.

DAY THIRTY-EIGHT

The [Step Four] inventory, though sometimes painful, unlocks many of the secrets that keep us prisoner and protect our addiction.
—*Twelve Steps for Tobacco Users*

Like many others, I had to have someone to blame for my addiction. "If he would only stop (fill in the blank) I could quit for good!" And so on. The trouble is I will always run into problems in my life that seem insurmountable. Until I realize I am powerless over other people, places and things, I am cut off from freedom.

Until I did a seriously thorough and courageous Step Four, looking at all of my struggles in life and sorting out which ones I helped cause, I could not be free. Freedom does indeed come from wholeheartedly working the Steps.

Like others I have resentments, misgivings, things that make me wish I were elsewhere or somebody else. If I faithfully turn to my Higher Power for the lifting of these grievances, I will get answers. Prayer, if given enough focus, can release me from the pain of my problems.

Today, although it is tough for me as an addict to refrain from blaming others, I take responsibility for my own actions.

DAY THIRTY-NINE

Many strokes will bring down the tallest tree.
—DAILY REFLECTIONS: A BOOK OF REFLECTIONS BY A.A. MEMBERS FOR A.A. MEMBERS

To help myself quit chewing, I made myself three easy goals to reach: Short, medium and long-range goals.

I started going one hour without nicotine, then two hours, and then the long-range goal of four hours. I did this several times a day.

As my need for nicotine lessened, I would increase my goals, first by doubling the hours, then by days, weeks, months, until I was free of my desire for nicotine one day at a time.

Today, I remember that when I keep it simple, I can achieve my goals.

DAY FORTY

The central fact of our lives today is the absolute certainty that our Creator has entered into our hearts and lives in a way which is indeed miraculous. He has commenced to accomplish those things for us which we could never do by ourselves.
—ALCOHOLICS ANONYMOUS

Giving anything up to my Higher Power was never an idea for me. But since I came to the rooms of Nicotine Anonymous, I have learned a new concept. I made a decision to turn my will and my life over to the care of God, as I understood Him, (Step Three).

One evening I was tired of feeling so bad and of coughing my head off every morning. I knew I had to do something. For me, the only way to quit using nicotine was to turn it over to my Higher Power. I was alone and had gotten rid of all nicotine items around me. I walked out to my pool. I held my hands up to my Higher Power. I prayed, "God, I'm powerless over nicotine. Please take the desire to smoke away. I have smoked for thirty-three years. I am powerless. Take it God." Then I jumped into my pool.

When I came up to the surface, I felt like a cleansing had happened and I felt deep inside of me that I really had no desire to smoke. Today and every day I am a grateful recovering nicotine addict, thanks to my Higher Power.

Today, instead of trying to figure things out by myself, I will try letting my Higher Power help me.

DAY FORTY-ONE

By the inch it's a cinch, by the yard it's hard.
—UNKNOWN

Lack of power—that was my dilemma. I was a slave to an addiction I had no control over. The answer to this dilemma lay in my admission that I could not overcome this situation with my own resources. I needed help.

Not only did I need help from God, as I understood Him, but also from my fellow nicotine addicts who understood my powerlessness. This was the key for me, not only vertical help but horizontal help also, forming a cross of victory.

Through attending meetings, working the Twelve Steps and helping others, I have discovered the freedom I so desperately sought. I know this is possible for others too.

Today, freedom is mine if I ask for help from the God of my understanding and from my fellow recovering addicts.

DAY FORTY-TWO

I am powerless over nicotine but not over my responsible choices.
—NICOTINE ANONYMOUS MEMBER

I am finding that life is like a puzzle with which I need to patiently and gently try to fit the many different pieces (choices) together, instead of thinking I have found the correct piece and forcing the fit. Forcing can distort and damage the entire puzzle (my life). Forcing the fit was my practice before I discovered Nicotine Anonymous, and my life was unmanageable. I actually thought nicotine helped me make good decisions as I contemplated them in a drugged fog.

And, now, when I tentatively try a piece of the puzzle that to all appearance (in my estimable judgment) is wrong, it invariably slides into place and the whole puzzle is improved and harmonious, and I feel even more happy, joyous and free.

This is why today I do not avoid or evade the inevitable puzzling circumstances of life. Instead, I welcome the challenge and am comfortable in the discomfort of seeking the right piece for the fitting solution, as I allow a power greater than I guide all my physical, mental, emotional and spiritual choices.

I am grateful that the daily polishing of my soul by practicing the Twelve Steps, Traditions and concepts in the fellowship of Nicotine Anonymous has led me away from my addiction that clouded my soul and interfered with my Higher Power's will for me.

Today, with the help of my Higher Power, I can make responsible choices.

DAY FORTY-THREE

Leap and the net will appear.
—JULIA CAMERON

When I tried to quit smoking, I would say things like, "well, I've cut down quite a bit," or "I am trying to quit," or "can I bum one of those, I am trying to quit?" I tried to control nicotine by not using it as much. I tried to manage life without nicotine. Of course, those attempts were just that. I tried to quit. Have you ever tried to pick up a piece of paper? You either pick it up or you do not. It is the same thing with nicotine: I am either using it or I am not.

I sat on my bed late one night and the thought popped into my head, "if you want to quit smoking, you have got to quit smoking." Those of us who are in the grip of nicotine addiction will not laugh at this simple realization.

This time I simply surrendered; I just stopped fighting it. This time I stopped dwelling on the time since the last cigarette. I did not actually quit. I mean, I was just done. I was sick and tired of trying to defeat, control, or manage life without nicotine. This time, I am not tense about it. No longer does nicotine have its deadly grasp on my soul. No, it is not as though I have given up anything at all; I have just surrendered.

Today, if I am swimming against the tide of a situation and finding myself exhausted from the effort, I will try letting go and floating on the surface of the tide instead.

DAY FORTY-FOUR

If the doors of perception were cleansed the world would appear as it is, infinite.
—WILLIAM BLAKE

Life is a gift from my Higher Power. I never understood that when I was smoking. There was a constant depression, a denial of what I was doing to my being, a self-destructiveness that negated the gift.

Now that I have moved over to the other side, from death to life, I see. I can value the gift and take care of it. Life is worth living. The depression lifts or at least lessens. Instead of destructive behavior, I behave in physically life-enhancing activities like running, biking, and swimming, or annual medical check ups, eating and sleeping well.

I do not know how to explain to a nicotine addict what is on the other side of the door of addiction. But, if the door can be opened enough to glimpse the totally new orientation to life that is on the other side, then hope rather than despair is possible. There is a new freedom that is more than freedom from nicotine but also a freedom from the negative orientation to life that is the addict's lot.

Go through the door. It will hurt. There will be demons, temptations, and midnight struggles. But a Higher Power and friends in this program will be there to help do what is impossible to do alone. I have heard the saying "Courage is fear that has said its prayers."

I have experienced a miracle.

Today, I will open the doors of my fears with courage and the support of my friends in the program.

DAY FORTY-FIVE

Make up your mind to act decidedly and take the consequences. No good is ever done in this world by hesitation.
— THOMAS HENRY HUXLEY

Like many others, I put off attempting to do anything about my nicotine addiction for years. I heard about things I could try; witnessed others who were able to stop. But I hesitated, "not yet, maybe someday." These words became all too familiar.

Hesitation can make an eternity out of a pause. Setting life on hold is part of a nicotine addict's pattern. I often lit up as a means to create a pause. I wanted to hold off the outside world or stuff my inside world.

Recovery encourages me to act decisively and to accept the consequences. This is being alive. Hesitation is like holding my breath; it approaches death. Each time I decide to act and accept the results, I am in the flow of life and therefore connected to its energy.

Today, cleared of the fog of addiction, I can respond consciously to my circumstances and be invigorated by this engagement.

DAY FORTY-SIX

"But" is a fence over which few leap.
—GERMAN PROVERB

Taking a moment and considering all the big and little things I have thought about doing during my life, but. . . . How many times have I put a "but" in my way and turned aside? How many times have I put a butt in my mouth and turned aside? And how many times have I felt like an ass or a butt because I turned and missed an opportunity?

Okay, let me take a good breath, this program is not about feeling more shame. Like many others I have been trying too long to numb myself from that. However, my buts list could be added to my Fourth Step inventory. The more I see where I turned away, the more I see where I need to head.

I want to live my life without any more ifs, ands, or buts . . . . or butts!

Today, I pray, may my detours be lifted so that I can move more freely towards my desires.

DAY FORTY-SEVEN

Fear is a tyrant and a despot, more terrible than the rack, more potent than the snake.
—Edgar Wallace

When I was a toddler, I climbed up on a desk, picked up my Dad's magazine, and leaned up against the screen to read it. The screen came loose, and I fell backwards out of the second story window. I have always been sure that caused my fear of heights. That fear kept me from doing things I thought looked like fun for others. I had to avoid things like ski lifts and hot air balloon rides. I always said that someday I would work on getting over my fear.

Then one day I realized that I affirmed my fear, gave it power and permanence, every time I said or thought, "I am afraid of heights." I changed and began affirming that I have released my fear. I bought a model of a hot air balloon, and put it in my office to remind me to affirm, "I am free to enjoy heights."

That's all I did. I did not go to a counselor to learn how to adjust to my fear, or to work through the panic. I simply affirmed my new freedom.

A few months later, I had the opportunity to test my freedom. I attended a banquet in the top floor of a skyscraper that had windows all the way to the floor. In the past I could not even walk into such a room. My husband challenged me to walk over to the window and look down. I affirmed my freedom, then I looked down. There was no panic, only a slight flutter. I chose to attribute the flutter to the awesome view.

Today, I acknowledge my feeling of fear; I decide whether the feeling is still useful to me, and if not, I gently release it, and affirm my new choice.

DAY FORTY-EIGHT

We are also beginning to love ourselves.
THE PROMISES OF NICOTINE ANONYMOUS

During the changing seasons it is apparent a Higher Power is at work in the world. I need to realize there is a Higher Power at work in me as well. I am a unique being to be cherished. I did not come off of some celestial assembly line but was made special and unique.

It is often too easy for me to see myself as unwanted goods. Whether it's because I have been hurt growing up or just have a low self-image I have been accustomed to think of myself as less than. That is one reason I used nicotine, to blot out the feelings of discomfort I felt in my own skin.

The beauty of the Twelve Steps is that they help me come to know myself again, in the way my Higher Power knows and loves me. I have found the best tool is the Step Four inventory. I was tempted to list only the areas I am lacking, but Step Four is truly meant to be a way to take stock of my whole self. I must not list only my liabilities; I must list my assets as well. I was surprised to find there are many. It is essential to know what a precious, unique person I am and to see my place in this wonderful creation.

Today I thank God for creating me as a unique and essential person. I love me as you love me.

DAY FORTY-NINE

We are as sick as our secrets.
—Twelve Step saying

One thing I have learned in Nicotine Anonymous is to be honest with myself and with each other. I learned to do this because I found that keeping secrets kept me sick and not making progress in recovery.

Like others it took me time to become entirely honest, but it was worth the effort. I do this by completing a Step Four inventory, and telling God and another human being my inner most secrets (Step Five). From this experience, I learned to be honest in life on a daily basis.

Now, when I start keeping secrets, I know I am deviating from my recovery and the Twelve Steps. Thoughts and behaviors I want to hide from friends and sponsors serve as a warning to me, threatening my recovery. If I cannot learn what is my truth and have the courage to accept it, I will become sick. My health is important to me, and the tools of the program help keep that a priority in my recovery.

Today, I remember that rigorous honesty is the best health insurance policy.

DAY FIFTY

This above all: to thine own self be true, and it must follow, as the night the day, thou canst not then be false to any man.
—SHAKESPEARE, *HAMLET*

Before I started coming to Nicotine Anonymous meetings, I was a very dishonest person. I wanted everyone to like me, so I pretended to agree with every thing they said. I would draw harder on my cigarette to keep from saying how I really felt.

When I quit smoking, I had no place for these feelings to go. I was very difficult and too blunt.

Because of Nicotine Anonymous, I learned to be honest and kind. I'm not perfect, however I am a much happier person. Being able to tell the truth with love makes me feel better about myself.

Today, I will remember that honesty brings serenity.

DAY FIFTY-ONE

To know even one life has breathed easier because you have lived, this is to have succeeded.
—RALPH WALDO EMERSON

I had to finally get honest. I really did not want to quit smoking. So I decided to ask my Higher Power for the willingness to want to quit.

My Higher Power granted me willingness quickly in the form of my inability to breathe and having to be rushed to the Emergency Room. The ER doctor said in front of my kids, "Did you know you're killing yourself in front of your kids? This is all cigarette-related. You wouldn't even be here if you didn't smoke."

My willingness came to me: I did not want to die. I did want to live. I became honest and in that honesty came freedom. It opened my eyes and heart to reality and gave me willingness to get help for myself. Thank goodness for my Higher Power and for honesty, as I am now a grateful recovering nicotine addict.

Today, I know that honesty can bring many rewards and one of those rewards is living without active addiction.

DAY FIFTY-TWO

Quitting smoking is the best gift you can give yourself!
—NICOTINE ANONYMOUS MEMBER

I am learning to be patient with myself. I am learning that it doesn't help to beat myself for all the years I smoked because I cannot bring them back. All I have is today.

I have learned to love myself, more than I have ever loved myself before. I do nice things for myself, like taking a walk no matter the weather, taking a bubble bath, eating well and getting a decent night's sleep, or eating vegetables with dip.

I am learning to listen, to open my ears. I heard people in nicotine anonymous meetings rooting for me. I can be an example too by not smoking! Living free of nicotine has not been a painless or easy journey, but it has been a road very worth taking.

Today, I will appreciate my gifts and carry the message by living by example.

DAY FIFTY-THREE

At the great heart of humanity, there is a deep homesickness that never has been and never can be satisfied with anything less than a clear, vivid consciousness of the indwelling presence of God.
— DR. EMILY CADY

When the craving for nicotine hits, what is it really about? If I really listen with my heart I begin to realize what it is saying to me.

Is it not really a craving for closeness and intimacy with others? Is it not a yearning to be spiritually one with a power greater than myself? And is it not a heartfelt plea to have a sense of belonging with others?

When the pain of craving comes, I choose to embrace myself instead of the spiritual death that comes from using nicotine.

Today, I will listen to what the craving is saying to me. I will not turn away from it; I will answer it. I will cultivate the courage to love.

DAY FIFTY-FOUR

Ever'thing there is but lovin' leaves a rust on yo' soul.
—LANGSTON HUGHES

When I was active in my nicotine use, I did not know myself. I measured my self-worth with the opinions of others, and as a result despised myself. Nicotine helped me with that. My drug kept me in my "dis-ease," kept me from experiencing my true self and the world around me. For a long time, that was very comforting. But slowly, initially in another Twelve Step program, I saw I could have more. I began to choose life and myself.

Nicotine Anonymous and the amazing people in the rooms became my Higher Power. From them I received unconditional love. With that secure base, I began, tentatively at first, to experience life without my drug. The amount of love and support I received encouraged me to try loving myself enough not to use nicotine.

Rust still lurks in the corners of my soul; I am still young in my recovery and always discovering something new about myself. But hour by hour, day by day, and through the love of this program, I am cleaning my rust away and replacing it with trust.

Today, I will choose love and faith over fear and mistrust.

DAY FIFTY-FIVE

The process of change is like planting a seed and watching it grow and bloom into a flower."
—MELODY BEATTIE

One of the miracles that happened when I quit using nicotine was that I learned to love myself. Without nicotine, I learned that I had choices and I began doing what I needed to do for myself. The road was not easy. I lost many friends along the way, friends who did not like who I was becoming. But I replaced those friends with people who genuinely love me for myself, not for what I am able to do for them.

I learned that using nicotine did not reduce stress in my life. It actually prolonged stress. Nicotine did not help me cope. Nicotine trapped me in unhealthy behavior. After I quit, I became more aware of my feelings and the choices available to me. I learned that going to meetings and doing service kept me from picking up nicotine, one day at a time.

I learned to set goals. Before Nicotine Anonymous I demanded instant gratification. Today, I am willing to wait and work towards my goals. What a wonderful feeling that is.

Today, I live in the present. I thank God I am free to make choices, set goals, and enjoy the present moment.

DAY FIFTY-SIX

I'm looking forward to today. There's a Nicotine Anonymous meeting this evening.
—NICOTINE ANONYMOUS MEMBER

Like many others in our program, I could quit on my own, but staying quit was impossible. Then I found Nicotine Anonymous.

Meetings were definitely the answer to my problem of addiction. Being with others, and sharing our experience, strength and hope turned my life around.

I thank God every day that I no longer have to feed my addiction. I thank God for the Nicotine Anonymous fellowship, because without this program I might return to living as an addict. I enjoy my life, and I want to keep it like it is, free of nicotine.

Today, I thank God for helping me live nicotine free one day at a time, for the rest of my life.

DAY FIFTY-SEVEN

The only thing we have to fear is fear itself—nameless, unreasoning, unjustified terror—which paralyzes needed efforts to convert retreat into advance.
—FRANKLIN D. ROOSEVELT

I treated feelings like facts, so the only way to find relief was through my nicotine addiction. You showed me the only power and reality behind my feelings is what I grant them. I learned to honor my feelings and to search for the lessons behind them. I learned to change what I could. I learned about boundaries, setting and enforcing my own, and respecting boundaries set by others for themselves.

Yesterday, I struggled to fight through fears. If something was hard, I just had to be tougher. Nicotine Anonymous taught me to, "Let Go and Let God." Today, I am learning to gently release fears in all areas of my life. I am learning to reinforce a new vision for myself, instead of fighting against the old behaviors.

Instead of affirming, "I am terrified to sing publicly," I affirm, "God gave me talent I am delighted to share." Instead of affirming, "I am terrified of heights," I affirm, "I am free to enjoy heights." All statements are expressions of feelings. None is a fact. I am free to choose the one I want for my truth.

Today, I take care in choosing the words that follow, "I am." I know those words will be my truth.

DAY FIFTY-EIGHT

It is never too late to become what you might have been.
—GEORGE ELIOT

One of the things I have noticed at Nicotine Anonymous meetings is how many people cough. And we all know about "smoker's cough." It's actually a good thing: it's our lungs trying desperately to clear themselves of all the toxins from cigarettes.

When I went to an annual Nicotine Anonymous conference, I noticed there was no coughing in the room. Some of those people have not had a cigarette in many years. How wonderful that we have that to look forward to!

Today, I thank my Higher Power for helping me to have healthy lungs.

DAY FIFTY-NINE

The only source of knowledge is experience.
—ALBERT EINSTEIN

Eventually the craving for nicotine begins to pass the further away I am from my quit date. I have gone through those intense emotions and I actually have begun to forget about nicotine sometimes. This is the time when I can be present, instead of wondering when the next hit will be.

The thing about "being present" is that I get to enjoy all the wonderful things that are happening around me every day.

Today, I take time to express my gratitude to my Higher Power. Thank you for easing my cravings and giving me the opportunity to experience life today.

DAY SIXTY

Teams share the burden and divide the grief.
—DOUG SMITH

Having been nicotine free for over eleven months, I was anxious to reach the one-year plateau. I continued to do the things that had gotten me to that point: asking God for help; talking with other addicts; going to meetings; and thanking God at night for another day of freedom from my addictions.

One night, however, I had a strange dream. In the dream someone gave me a few dollars to get them something. I went to the store and bought a pack of cigarettes for myself. Without another thought I returned to my "friend." Only then did I realize what I had done. Now, I did not smoke any cigarettes, but I was awed at the ease and thoughtlessness with which I had purchased them.

The dream made me think how that kind of thing had happened to other members, some with a lot of clean time, who had gone back to nicotine with little or no forethought at all. Or of some who had mistakenly convinced themselves that they could just have one. I must always remember that it is not how much clean time I have; it is staying clean today; and today is so very, very precious.

Today, I ask God to guide me and strengthen me to stay clean just for these twenty-four hours.

DAY SIXTY-ONE

We don't know exactly how our dream will be accomplished. We don't even know if it's probable. But we can believe that with God's help it is possible.
—MARY MANNIN MORRISSEY

I was down and out, in a lot of trouble physically and mentally. There was no way that continuing to smoke was going to work for me.

My doctors warned me about lung cancer. They removed part of my lung. I still had a desire to smoke. Instead, I went back to Nicotine Anonymous where I received encouragement from my group.

Today, I do not need to smoke and have no desire to. I keep going to meetings. Maybe my story will help somebody. I will always be grateful to my local meeting and the program because I was told to "keep coming back" and that the program would eventually "get" me. It did!

Today, I ask myself what I can do to give back to my meeting.

DAY SIXTY-TWO

You are the only person God had in mind in choosing you to be you.
—REV. JOEL HUGHES

For so many years, I punished myself for smoking and for being so helpless over the addiction, making myself feel puny and worthless. For years I would mentally beat myself up. Even with years in recovery, if I am not careful, I still punish myself. I do not beat myself up about smoking anymore, but about other imagined imperfections.

"Be good to yourself," I heard people I met saying at meetings. "Rejoice in all the good we do and know that we are trying our best." I have learned that if I make it through today nicotine-free my day is a success. And that I have Step Ten to help make amends when needed.

I am learning to reward myself: a two week vacation in Hawaii paid for with money not spent on nicotine for one year; some quiet time with the God of my understanding; feeling gratitude for being alive and nicotine-free; staying after Nicotine Anonymous meetings and visiting with people; being a sponsor; being sponsored. Even though being good to myself seems hard to do, when I need it the most, it is so important and freeing and it makes me smile.

Today, I will remember that I am not intended to be perfect. Throughout the day I will find ways to reward myself and be good to myself.

DAY SIXTY-THREE

The deepest need of man is the need to overcome his separateness, to leave the prison of his aloneness.
—ERICH FROMM

Peer pressure, the loneliness of low self-esteem, and the sexual enticement alluded to in movies all played a part in my early encounters with using nicotine. As a young person I was trying to develop an identity and a relationship with the world. Like others, I did this awkwardly, often foolishly, sometimes even desperately.

A youth wants to be somebody important enough to have a connection with a group. To be denied this is painful; a living death to some. With the focus on tobacco instead of on my insecure self, I could bond more easily with my peers. I could light up and be let in.

One of the strengths of a recovery program is that each member is important and useful. There is a bonding through the courage to show up. With sharing, the bond grows. Those still using nicotine keep the danger fresh for those who have put the drug down. Those who are clean offer hope to those who aspire. Recovery becomes our new connection. We bond in celebrating our dream, living free of nicotine.

Today, any sense of aloneness is comforted by a fellowship of support and contact with a Higher Power.

DAY SIXTY-FOUR

He that will believe only what he can fully comprehend must have a very long head or a very short creed.
— C. C. COLTON

In this program of recovery I heard that miracles happen. As a newcomer, I was skeptical of the idea. Like other nicotine addicts I needed a long time before I was ready to admit I needed the help of a recovery program. I had become accustomed to an instant solution I could hold in my hands. The notion of accepting a reality I could not grasp was beyond me, at first.

The more time I spend clean, the clearer I see the world around me. With the veil of nicotine gone I can witness more of Nature's beauty. I smell it, taste it, and touch it. I can now celebrate the creation. I am no longer trying to hide from this marvel called life. My first miracle may be that I stopped using nicotine, but this was only the beginning of my amazement.

Today, I am learning to embrace miracles.

DAY SIXTY-FIVE

Unhappy is the man, though he rules the world, who doesn't consider himself supremely blest.
—SENECA

How easy it is to forget all that I have to be grateful for. If a sunrise and sunset were a once-a-year occurrence, it would be a national holiday. Businesses and schools would be closed, and everyone would plan to be with the people they love, in the place they love. No doubt about it, it would be a grand day for celebration!

How often do I remember to be grateful? I am grateful that my nicotine addiction is no longer active. I am grateful I am no longer driven to buy and use that drug. It's so easy when I'm annoyed, or disappointed, or hungry-angry-lonely-tired (HALT), to forget that I'm free of nicotine for today and very grateful to my Higher Power for this program and the people in it.

If I forget to be grateful, Higher Power, give me a little nudge—a beautiful sunrise, sunset, a glorious day, a call from a friend, an enthusiastic hello from my pet, an empty pack of cigarettes on the ground that isn't mine.

Today, I pause to be grateful. I know that an attitude of gratitude will keep me free.

DAY SIXTY-SIX

I can use nicotine if I want to, but for this very moment, I choose not to.
—NICOTINE ANONYMOUS MEMBER

One of my reasons for using nicotine was to help me relax, little did I know. Since I quit fueling my addiction, I have been helped tremendously by finding new and healthier means of relaxation. A few of my favorites are bicycling, stretching, taking a yoga class, creating arts and crafts, and meditating.

Now that I am on the road to recovery, I am rediscovering what I like doing and what brings me peace. Perhaps my favorite stress reliever of all is my monthly massage. When compared to the money I used to spend on nicotine, a massage once a month sure feels like a softer, easier way.

Today, I acknowledge the depths of the pain and despair that nicotine brought me, and although it may feel scary, just for today I choose not to use any form of nicotine.

DAY SIXTY-SEVEN

He who is being carried does not realize how far the town is.
—NIGERIAN PROVERB

During my years of active nicotine addiction, I did not know the many experiences and the thousands of feelings I was blunting by staying drugged. Because it was legal and it was socially acceptable at the time, I had no awareness that I was zoning out, literally being carried through life without facing my emotions.

Today I no longer live behind that nicotine fog. Today I am free to feel and to experience all that life has to offer. Living life on life's terms is not easy and I have needed the help of Nicotine Anonymous. But today I do see how far the town is and I am not dependent on nicotine to carry me there. I know that my Higher Power will show me the way. Today I trust my feelings instead of hiding from them.

Today, I rely on Nicotine Anonymous to show me how to live without drug dependency. I rely on my Higher Power and
trust my own feelings.

DAY SIXTY-EIGHT

"Without the acquisition of another skill, without the acquisition of anything but complete and total trust in God and in yourself, you have everything you need to interact optimally, creatively and productively with every situation you encounter."
—KEN CAREY

Oh God of my understanding I pray, please give me whatever I need to live this life free of tobacco.

For me tobacco is a poison I became addicted to. It ran my life. I ask You, God, please help and guide me one day at a time in my efforts to live free of my deadly addiction. This is the same addiction that killed my mother in such an agonizing way. I truly believe in the core of my being that Your will for me is to live free of the drug nicotine that I used for so many years. Thank you God for each and every moment free of the compulsion to feed my addiction.

Today, I know I can live free of nicotine as long as I accept the help freely given to me by my Higher Power.

DAY SIXTY-NINE

Take a deep breath. Usually, we anticipate something to follow that is painful, like a shot. Or maybe someone is asking us to calm down. How about just for today, you say to yourself, "take a deep breath." You don't have to have a reason. What a blessing a deep breath is. —REV. JOEL HUGHES

Whenever I had to meet with people I did not know, I always felt compelled to feed my nicotine addiction. As soon as I had the first hit, my feeling of fear was subdued. I felt more prepared to make acquaintances.

It bothered me that I had to depend on nicotine to make me feel normal, to shrink my fear to a manageable level.

By coming to meetings and working the Steps, I learned to love myself. As I learned to love myself, I released my fear of meeting new people. I also learned that not everyone will like me, and that's OK.

Today, I thank God for lifting my fears and allowing me to meet people without a drug.

DAY SEVENTY

Sought through prayer and meditation to improve my conscious contact with God as I understand Him.
—STEP ELEVEN

Practicing my daily meditation is very important to me, but it's not always easy. I get a little annoyed sometimes. "Yup! Okay! I get it. Time to gently release the thought and bring my attention back to my breathing, again!" Ugh!

Today, my mind was diving and tunneling and leaping all over the map. It reminded of the way my cats love to jump suddenly and dart around. I was watching my mind frolic and play. My face broke out into a big stupid grin, and I started laughing under my breath. If you have done much meditating in groups, or if you have spent any time talking to your best friend in school during class, you will know what it was like. It was great to stop taking myself so seriously, and to let meditating be fun.

For me, that was enlightenment, to notice how funny I can be, and to laugh at myself. I decided that, "the sound of one hand clapping" is the sound of my hand clapping over my mouth to stifle my laughter. Maybe Bodhidarma would not have approved, but it was good enough for me.

Nicotine Anonymous has taught me that surrender allows change. If I keep showing up and working my program, my life just keeps getting better.

Today, I thank God for life's everyday pleasures, and for granting me the wisdom to see them.

DAY SEVENTY-ONE

Take a deep breath: it helps you pay attention. It's the miracle of our lives....

There are always miracles going on, all we have to do is look for them.

—Jay L.

Pausing in our hectic day to just take a breath and to pay attention helps reduce stress and remind us that our Higher Power is ever present. A deep breath is a miracle, as are so many things that are in our lives: a flower, a bee, and a blade of grass. Sometimes just stopping to pay attention is all we need to see the miracles around us, and to experience the miracle of a deep breath.

Today, Higher Power, thank you for all the miracles that happen every day.

DAY SEVENTY-TWO

Our spiritual life is a reality, not a theory.... It is something each of us must invent for ourselves: it is experiential.
—UNKNOWN

Being in Nicotine Anonymous and doing the Twelve Steps is a spiritual path. It is one of the tools of our recovery. We need to bring our spirituality into our lives every day so that we are connected to our Higher Power and through our Higher Power to the Universe. Spirituality is very practical and down-to-earth. We connect with it when we pause to breathe, when someone is kind to us, when we look at the stars at night or plant a seed and watch it grow. We connect with it at Nicotine Anonymous meetings.

Today, I will remember my connection to a Power greater than myself.

DAY SEVENTY-THREE

We have enormous power in knowing the truth of our own experience.
—ANITA HILL

I stopped using nicotine because I knew it was killing me. My friends and family may have tried to get me to quit, but until I was ready, it was not going to happen. Sometimes my addict friends do not believe I will stay quit. I have to trust my own experience and my own Higher Power in regard to my addiction.

Today, I trust my own experience and use it as a teacher in working with my addiction.

DAY SEVENTY-FOUR

The craving will pass whether you smoke or not.
—NICOTINE ANONYMOUS MEMBER

I can remember when I was a nicotine user. I would always say to myself, "One more and then I will go to bed, one more and then I'll go to sleep." A half a pack later, I would finally go to bed without a thought of what I must smell like, or that I just washed my hair and brushed my teeth. I never thought of my poor, non-smoking husband.

Today, I cannot stand the smell of smoke. I can tell a smoker if they walk past me, even if they are not smoking.

Since coming to Nicotine Anonymous I finally have self-respect. I finally have what I needed, a group of people who want to share about nicotine addiction.

Today, I ask you, Lord, help me stay nicotine free. Thank you for restoring my senses.

DAY SEVENTY-FIVE

I no longer search for "truth." I search only for beliefs that serve me, that help me to get where I truly want to go. Then I work diligently at discarding beliefs that work against me.
— BARRY NEIL KAUFMAN

For me, the best gift of recovery is a true and honest relationship with God as I understand God. I struggled with that before recovery. I lived my life alone with no spiritual connections of any personal meaning. And then people in recovery suggested that I develop my own concept of God.

On a good day I do as suggested in our Twelve Steps, praying only for God's will and the power (and willingness) to carry that out. Not smoking or using nicotine, I believe, is God's will for me, as well as trying in my own ways to carry the message of recovery.

To me, God is my partner in life. I do not claim to understand who God is or how God works. This great mystery is my partner, my guide, and my trusted helper.

Today, I pray for and act in the faith that God wants me to be happy, joyous and free.

DAY SEVENTY-SIX

You will love again the stranger who was yourself.
— DEREK WALCOTT

By the time I had smoked for thirty years I had pretty much lost contact with who I really was. Anything genuine about me had long been buried under a blanket of cigarette smoke.

Even now, as I begin to see more clearly, I realize that many of my earlier loves were put aside, everything from poetry to bowling, so that I could make room for how I ought to be. Using nicotine helped me do that.

Freedom from nicotine has led to greater freedom in all aspects of living. Old interests have been revived and new ones found as well.

Today, my goal in life is to become the best person I am capable of being.

DAY SEVENTY-SEVEN

Your end is your beginning, you start when you finish.
—***RAMAYANA**,* (TRANSLATED) BY WILLIAM BUCK

After thirty years of addiction, and seven years nicotine free, I still remember my last smoke. I remember frantically smoking that butt before a Nicotine Anonymous meeting, and burning my lip in the process.

I can think of nothing positive that came from all those years of smoking. I have truly had an awakening, a new way of life. Since then I have been living each day, one day at a time, without nicotine.

It is refreshing to end one chapter, and to begin another. Having ended my smoking career, I discovered a full and rewarding life awaiting me, with no place for nicotine.

Today, I no longer have time to feed my nicotine addiction. I am free to enjoy all of life's pleasures.

DAY SEVENTY-EIGHT

All our life is but the blink of an eye.
—***RAMAYANA***, TRANSLATED BY WILLIAM BUCK

I think of all the people who have gone before us on this earth, and yet it is as if they were never here at all. They left no lasting impression. I think back to when I was actively practicing my addiction; it was the same with me; I was not really here at all.

Among the many gifts of the program has been a greater awareness and appreciation for the daily experience of what is life. I no longer have to buffer this experience with the drug of nicotine.

Seeing things more clearly, as they truly are and not as I would like them, continues to be a challenge, one that can be lived best without nicotine.

Today, I simply appreciate each unfolding moment of life.

DAY SEVENTY-NINE

Show up, pay attention, tell the truth and don't be attached to the outcome.
—Angeles Arrien

As the winter solstice approaches and the days become shorter, I am reminded of the darkness that seemed to grip me with increasing strength in the final days of my active addiction: the social ostracism; the fear, anxiety and worry over the harm I was causing myself physically; the utter hopelessness I felt about ever being able to quit.

I feared living without my constant companion. I anticipated that life without nicotine would be impossible. But the solstice teaches me that this projection was unwarranted. Just when it seems the darkness will never end, there comes a turning point when the days become longer and warmer. Just as I anticipated that life would be unbearable without nicotine, recovery teaches me that life can be filled with so much goodness, beyond my wildest dreams.

Today, I choose to live in anticipation that light inevitably follows darkness.

DAY EIGHTY

I no longer count the value of a day by feeling the change in my pocket, but by feeling the change in my heart.
—NICOTINE ANONYMOUS MEMBER

When we are children, much of how good we feel depends on what we get. Whether it's attentive care, birthday presents, or just getting our way, our focus is on getting something from the outside world. We continually count our marbles and feel powerful, satisfied, or resentful when we compare our pile to others.

Many of us became addicts when we were still children, often starting with nicotine. We may have wanted to get away with or get more, but found we could never get enough.

In recovery we learn about the tool of service and carrying the message by practicing the program's principles, such as humility, kindliness, and patience "in all our affairs." Maturity comes when we realize our real value comes from what we have to offer and freely give it away.

Today, I will count my blessings and offer them to others, knowing this is the source of true wealth.

DAY EIGHTY-ONE

When you're away, I'm restless, lonely, wretched, bored, dejected; only here's the rub my darling dear, I feel the same when you are near.
—SAMUEL HOFFENSTEIN

How I missed my little tobacco "friends" when I first stopped putting them into my mouth. I felt deprived and abandoned. These are very common experiences when we first let go. Even when I was still using, just the anticipation of being deprived was enough to keep me from attempting to quit.

After some time in recovery, I accepted that I had felt restless, lonely, wretched, bored, dejected even before I quit. Once, I used the drug to numb these feelings—and may even have been unaware of *what* I was feeling. With recovery I discovered a full range of feelings. Some are new. Some are just more intense. Often they visit unexpectedly.

The support and the common bond I developed in our Fellowship help me come to know that I have gained and not lost "friends." The Twelve Steps help guide me so I can handle and enjoy this fuller life.

Today, I'm grateful to know what I'm feeling so that I can respond and attend to it in a sane and healthy manner.

DAY EIGHTY-TWO

What we have done is the only mirror by which we can see who we are.
—THOMAS CARLYLE

Living free of tobacco addiction is the most important thing in my life. My life and my health depend on this. It is so vitally important for my spiritual growth, my physical being, my self-esteem, and my emotional center. I do not want to waste my life and my money by continuing an addiction that kills and maims addicts in the prime of our lives, and cuts us off from each other and our Higher Power.

Oh God, please help me live the Twelve Steps. Help me seek help for myself. Help me give help to other addicts. Help me truly live this life, as You would have me live it. I pray to live one day at a time doing the next right thing. Working our Twelve Steps helps me avoid physical, emotional and spiritual death, and I am grateful.

Today I know all that God asks is that I do the next right thing.

Day: Eighty-three

Free at last, free at last. Thank, God Almighty, I'm free at last.
—Martin Luther King, Jr.

I used to believe I was free. I had learned to let go of other addictions. Then one day I realized my nicotine use was another addiction. Using nicotine was cutting me off from a true and personal relationship with God, a relationship based on freedom.

I had tried to quit since high school. I was varsity football and basketball, but could not run the one-mile track event because of my breathing. From age sixteen to fifty-eight, I attempted to quit many times, using many different methods, but never could stop for very long.

Then, I remembered the Twelve Step solution that had freed me from other addictions. I thought that maybe I could quit by applying those same principles to nicotine. Gathering the available information, I started a meeting for nicotine addicts on March 16, 1987, the date of my last cigarette. Nicotine Anonymous truly set me free. I now really know what Martin Luther King, Jr. meant.

Today, I thank God for guiding me to true freedom.

DAY EIGHTY-FOUR

A moment's insight is sometimes worth a life's experience.
—OLIVER WENDELL HOLMES

My part in recovery from nicotine addiction is and has been minimal compared to the part played by my Higher Power. My part was seeking, finding, calling on that Power, and acknowledging its source. I had proven I was powerless over my addiction by smoking three packs daily for forty-three years.

I had watched other addicts recover using Twelve Step programs. I knew the Steps worked, and that God blesses those who sincerely try to live the Steps. I consulted God about His plans for me, and asked Him to direct some Power my way if His plans would be helped by my not smoking. I agreed to cooperate with the miracle by being willing to use any available aids. I agreed when we were successful that I would let everyone know about this special stop-smoking Power.

Recently I celebrated two years of a life free of nicotine. Just for fun, I have the opportunity to share my experience, strength and hope with others in the Nicotine Anonymous fellowship.

Today, I thank God for the courage to change what I can, and the wisdom to rely on God for the rest.

DAY EIGHTY-FIVE

Having had a spiritual awakening as the result of these steps, we tried to carry this message to nicotine users and to practice these principles in all our affairs.
—STEP TWELVE

I was sitting in the lounge of another Twelve Step program when a lady I knew posted a flier on the bulletin board. The flier asked the question, "Do you want to stop smoking?"

Not only did I want to stop smoking, I wanted to be able to stay stopped. I had stopped smoking over and over, only to return to the habit and addiction one more time.

I decided to go to the meeting. I wanted to be able to say I was a former smoker when I introduced myself for the first time, so I was nicotine free for three days before the meeting. Through this program, I learned to continue to live nicotine free. Now I carry the message to other nicotine addicts who still suffer.

Today, I allow life to flow through me, and to bless others and myself.

DAY EIGHTY-SIX

The best way out is always through.
—ROBERT FROST

Nicotine Anonymous has given me the desire to get well and to overcome my addiction. It gives me a sense of safety, a sense of fellowship and belonging.

Since I arrived at my first Nicotine Anonymous meeting, I haven't fed my addiction. When I first heard, "keep coming back," my response was, "you betcha."

I love to share my experience, strength and hope with others. I also love to hear others share theirs. By going to meeting on a regular basis, I have learned to live life without my drug of choice, nicotine.

Whenever I see a newcomer at a meeting, I introduce myself, make sure they have a schedule of meetings, and always remind them to "keep coming back."

Today, I thank God for the program and the fellowship that encourages me to keep coming back.

DAY EIGHTY-SEVEN

As long as you keep showing up, you haven't given up.
—UNKNOWN

Fellowship with other recovering nicotine addicts demonstrates the presence of a loving Higher Power. At meetings people welcomed me every time I showed up, even while I was still active in my addiction. They understood my struggle. They did not judge or criticize. They hugged me and smiled. They told me to keep coming back.

It was their love and understanding that gave me the strength to keep getting back in my car and coming to meetings even when I felt hopeless. Their voices in my head, my memory of their warmth and caring, are what enabled me to pick up the telephone and call for help. Whether it was to seek help when I was craving a cigarette, or to confess that I had failed again, or to get support so I would resist picking up, there was always someone who had the time to talk.

I kept coming back, and today I am free of the compulsion to feed my nicotine addiction.

Today, I will accept each person I encounter with the unconditional love I have learned in our program.

DAY EIGHTY-EIGHT

I must be an addict because after sixteen years of not smoking, I become very angry when I am in a room with smokers!
—NICOTINE ANONYMOUS MEMBER

Sometimes I think that I am not addicted to the nicotine in cigarettes. After all, I did not start smoking until I was forty years old, and stopped after ten years. Okay, it took three attempts to quit during that decade.

The first time I relapsed I smoked for six months; the second relapse lasted thirteen months. The third time I quit smoking, I made it to my first Nicotine Anonymous meeting at that critical time of six months. That was three years ago!

What reminds me that I am an addict is that smokers fascinate me! When I see someone smoking in a car or on the street, I want a cigarette. Then I hear the honesty of another member sharing and I remember that I am an addict and I have a daily reprieve.

I keep coming back to remember I am an addict.

Today, I thank God I recognize my addiction and am willing to choose to abstain from feeding that addiction.

DAY EIGHTY-NINE

People who work together will win, whether it be against complex football defenses, or the problems of modern society.
—Vince Lombardi

Over twenty years ago, the last thing I wanted to do was to go to Alcoholic Anonymous meetings. I thought I could handle it on my own. I found out that I could not do it on my own. But I went. Alcoholics Anonymous has given me nineteen years of sobriety. Thank God and the program.

When I wanted to quit using nicotine, for some dumb unknown reason, the last thing I wanted to do was to go to a Nicotine Anonymous meeting. So, on January 1, 2001 I quit again. I lasted about two weeks. On March 25, 2001 I stopped again, this time using Nicotine Anonymous.

The programs are the same, only different. I gave my nicotine addiction to God. The craving has disappeared. The urge to use nicotine will stay away if I continue going to meetings. Quitting using nicotine has been the frosting on my cake.

Today, I am sensitive to resistance. If I feel resistance, I will stop to consider what I need to release or what support I require.

DAY NINETY

Freedom has many facets, but mostly it releases us from much that has been troubling and defeating us. We pray for this release into freedom.
—*One Day At A Time in Al-Anon*

When I was smoking, I thought that I was in control, but really it was the cigarette, really the nicotine in the cigarette, that was controlling me. Nicotine determined with whom I would travel, who would travel with me, even whether I would travel at all. Nicotine determined with whom I had relationships, and who would have them with me. It was these two themes around which my Higher Power led me back to Nicotine Anonymous. I was planning a trip to the South of France. The trip would involve not smoking for nine hours on the plane, and later traveling with non-smoking relatives. What complete and utter misery!

I was desperate and no longer wanted to suffer. In the rooms of Nicotine Anonymous, I found unconditional love, open arms, and the freedom to discover myself without the smothering blanket of nicotine. The people in the rooms held me as I learned to accept my powerlessness and not act on my cravings. I grabbed onto service as if it were a life preserver. I took lots of tools with me on my trip and did not smoke. I was able to experience many joyful moments as a result.

At the time of this writing, I am celebrating my fifth anniversary of freedom from nicotine, one day at a time. It is a miracle beyond my wildest dreams, and I could not have done it alone. I owe this day to Nicotine Anonymous.

Today, I will leave behind yesterday, not fear tomorrow, and live in the freedom of today.

The Twelve Steps of Nicotine Anonymous

1. We admitted we were powerless over nicotine—that our lives had become unmanageable.
2. Came to believe that a Power greater than ourselves could restore us to sanity.
3. Made a decision to turn our will and our lives over to the care of God, as we understood Him.
4. Made a searching and fearless moral inventory of ourselves.
5. Admitted to God, to ourselves, and to another human being the exact nature of our wrongs.
6. Were entirely ready to have God remove all these defects of character.
7. Humbly asked Him to remove our shortcomings.
8. Made a list of all persons we had harmed, and became willing to make amends to them all.
9. Made direct amends to such people wherever possible, except when to do so would injure them or others.
10. Continued to take personal inventory, and when we were wrong, promptly admitted it.
11. Sought through prayer and meditation to improve our conscious contact with God as we understood Him, praying only for knowledge of His will for us and the power to carry it out.
12. Having had a spiritual awakening as the result of these steps, we tried to carry this message to other nicotine users and to practice these principles in all our affairs.

The Twelve Steps reprinted and adapted here with the permission of Alcoholics Anonymous World Services, Inc. Permission to reprint and adapt the Twelve Steps does not mean that A.A. is affiliated with this program. A.A. is a program of recovery from alcoholism—use of the Twelve Steps in connection with programs and activities which are patterned after A.A., but which address other problems, does not imply otherwise.

The Twelve Steps of Alcoholics Anonymous

1. We admitted we were powerless over alcohol—that our lives had become unmanageable. 2. Came to believe that a Power greater than ourselves could restore us to sanity. 3. Made a decision to turn our will and our lives over to the care of God, as we understood Him. 4. Made a searching and fearless moral inventory of ourselves. 5. Admitted to God, to ourselves, and to another human being the exact nature of our wrongs. 6. Were entirely ready to have God remove all these defects of character. 7. Humbly asked Him to remove our shortcomings. 8. Made a list of all persons we had harmed, and became willing to make amends to them all. 9. Made direct amends to such people wherever possible, except when to do so would injure them or others. 10. Continued to take personal inventory, and when we were wrong, promptly admitted it. 11. Sought through prayer and meditation to improve our conscious contact with God as we understood Him, praying only for knowledge of His will for us and the power to carry it out. 12. Having had a spiritual awakening as the result of these steps, we tried to carry this message to other alcoholics and to practice these principles in all our affairs.

The Twelve Traditions of Nicotine Anonymous

1. Our common welfare should come first; personal recovery depends upon Nicotine Anonymous unity.
2. For our group purpose there is but one ultimate authority - a loving God as He may express Himself in our group conscience. Our leaders are but trusted servants; they do not govern.
3. The only requirement for Nicotine Anonymous membership is a desire to stop using nicotine.
4. Each group should be autonomous except in matters affecting other groups or Nicotine Anonymous as a whole.
5. Each group has but one primary purpose - to carry its message to the nicotine addict who still suffers.
6. A Nicotine Anonymous group ought never endorse, finance, or lend the Nicotine Anonymous name to any related facility or outside enterprise, lest problems of money, property, and prestige divert us from our primary purpose.
7. Every Nicotine Anonymous group ought to be fully self-supporting, declining outside contributions.
8. Nicotine Anonymous should remain forever non-professional, but our service centers may employ special workers.
9. Nicotine Anonymous, as such, ought never be organized; but we may create service boards or committees directly responsible to those they serve.
10. Nicotine Anonymous has no opinion on outside issues; hence the Nicotine Anonymous name ought never be drawn into public controversy.
11. Our public relations policy is based on attraction rather than promotion; we need always maintain personal anonymity at the level of press, radio, TV, and films.
12. Anonymity is the spiritual foundation of all our traditions, ever reminding us to place principles before personalities.

Copyright 1990, 1992 by Nicotine Anonymous The Twelve Traditions reprinted and adapted with permission of Alcoholics Anonymous World Services, Inc. Permission to reprint and adapt the Twelve Traditions does not mean that AA is affiliated with this program. AA is a program of recovery from alcoholism—use of the Twelve Traditions in connection with programs and activities which are patterned after AA, but which address other problems, does not imply otherwise. See Alcoholics Anonymous' Twelve Traditions below.

The Twelve Traditions of Alcoholics Anonymous

1. Our common welfare should come first; personal recovery depends upon A.A. unity. 2. For our group purpose there is but one ultimate authority—a loving God as He may express Himself in our group conscience. Our leaders are but trusted servants; they do not govern. 3. The only requirement for A.A. membership is a desire to stop drinking. 4. Each group should be autonomous except in matters affecting other groups or A.A. as a whole. 5. Each group has but one primary purpose - to carry the message to the alcoholic who still suffers. 6. An A.A. group ought never endorse, finance, or lend the A.A. name to any related facility or outside enterprise, lest problems of money, property, and prestige divert us from our primary purpose. 7. Every A.A. group ought to be fully self-supporting, declining outside contributions. 8. Alcoholics Anonymous should remain forever non-professional, but our service centers may employ special workers. 9. A.A., as such, ought never be organized; but we may create service boards or committees directly responsible to those they serve. 10. Alcoholics Anonymous has no opinion on outside issues; hence the A.A. name ought never be drawn into public controversy. 11. Our public relations policy is based on attraction rather than promotion; we need always maintain personal anonymity at the level of press, radio, and films. 12. Anonymity is the spiritual foundation of all our traditions, ever reminding us to place principles before personalities.

Copyright 1939, 1955, 1976 by Alcoholics Anonymous World Services, Inc.

Index

acceptance, iii, 1, 4, 21, 32
action, 1
addict, 4, 12, 16, 26, 31, 32, 35, 37, 38, 40, 44, 45, 51, 56, 73, 88
addicted, 6, 8, 9, 12, 68, 88
addiction, 2, 4, 8, 10, 12, 13, 15, 16, 20, 23, 24, 25, 26, 28, 30, 31, 35, 36, 37, 38, 41, 42, 43, 44, 45, 51, 56, 57, 62, 65, 66, 67, 68, 69, 73, 74, 77, 78, 79, 82, 83, 84, 85, 86, 87, 88, 89
addicts, 2, 3, 19, 24, 37, 41, 60, 64, 80, 82, 83, 84, 85, 87
amends, 28, 62
anger, 18, 28
angry, 18
anxiety, 79
assets, 48
attitude, 2, 20, 65
awareness, 67

bond, 63, 81
bored, 81
boundaries, 28, 57
breath, 12, 21, 35, 45, 46, 69, 70, 71
breathe, 12, 13, 15, 29, 51, 72
bronchitis, 13, 14, 29

celebrating, 63, 64
change, 4, 11, 13, 18, 22, 23, 32, 55, 57, 70, 80, 84
chewing, 15, 39
choice, 2, 7, 16, 19, 21, 37, 42, 47, 55, 86
comfort, 18
conflicts, 27
control, 6, 9, 20, 21, 22, 24, 25, 28, 32, 41, 43, 90
coughing, 14, 29, 35, 40, 58
courage, 24, 32, 44, 49, 53, 63, 84
craving, 11, 13, 16, 17, 24, 25, 36, 53, 59, 74, 87, 89

defects, 4
denial, 44
dependency, 67
depression, 44
detoxifying, 5
dream, 31, 37, 60, 61, 63
dreams, 2, 31, 79, 90

Easy Does It, 15; *see also* Slogans
effort, 43
emotions, 28, 34, 59, 67
emphysema, 13
excuses, 4

experience, 11
Experience, Strength and Hope, 17, 20, 56, 84, 86; *see also* Slogans

failures, 23
faith, 17
fear, 3, 26, 31, 44, 47, 54, 57, 69, 79, 90
feelings, 4, 13, 15, 16, 21, 48, 50, 55, 57, 67, 81
fellowship, 6, 13, 22, 23, 42, 56, 81, 84, 86, 87
focus, 21, 38, 63, 80
Fourth Step, 46
free will, 19
freedom, 1, 20, 22, 24, 35, 37, 38, 41, 44, 47, 51, 60, 76, 83, 90
frustrated, 18

gave up, 17
gift, 2, 20, 26, 37, 44, 52, 75
goals, 39, 55
grateful, 6, 8, 17, 36, 37, 40, 42, 51, 61, 65, 81, 82
gratitude, 20, 59, 62, 65
group, 5, 9, 17, 19, 30, 31, 61, 63, 70, 74
growth, 11
guidance, 2, 6, 18, 19, 35

HALT (Hungry, Angry, Lonely, Tired), 65
Happy, Joyous and Free, 12, 27, 42, 75; *see also* Slogans
healing, 4
health, 13, 14, 37, 49, 82
hesitation, 45
Higher Power, 3, 4, 5, 6, 7, 10, 11, 14, 17, 18, 19, 20, 21, 22, 23, 30, 32, 34, 35, 36, 37, 38, 40, 42, 44, 48, 51, 54, 58, 59, 63, 65, 67, 68, 71, 72, 73, 82, 84, 87, 90
hoax, 9, 26
honest, 27, 49, 50, 51, 75
hope, 9, 17, 20, 44, 56, 63, 84, 86
humiliated, 3
humility, 80
hungry, angry, lonely, tired, *see* HALT

insane, 13, 35
insanity, 4, 35
insecure, 63
intimacy, 53
inventory, 38

Keep Coming Back, 30, 61, 86, 87, 88, 95; see also Slogans
Keep It Simple, 39, 95; *see also* Slogans

Let Go and Let God, 5, 18, 36, 57; see also Slogans
letting go, 43
lies, 8
Life on Life's Terms, 32, 67; *see*

also Slogans
literature, 20
love, 1, 8, 15, 17, 18, 21, 31, 48, 50, 52, 53, 54, 55, 65, 69, 70, 76, 86, 87, 90
low self-image, 48

maturity, 80
meditating, 7, 21, 66, 70
meetings, 3, 6, 9, 13, 20, 23, 29, 30, 41, 50, 52, 55, 56, 58, 60, 61, 62, 69, 72, 86, 87, 89
miracle, 6, 20, 36, 37, 44, 55, 64, 71, 84, 90
my thinking, 1

newcomer, 64
next right thing, 82
Nicotine Anonymous, iii, iv, 2, 3, 5, 6, 7, 8, 9, 10, 12, 13, 14, 16, 17, 19, 24, 26, 29, 30, 31, 34, 35, 36, 40, 42, 48, 49, 50, 52, 54, 55, 56, 57, 58, 61, 62, 66, 67, 70, 72, 74, 77, 80, 83, 84, 86, 88, 89, 90

obsession, 7
One Day At a Time, 6, 7, 11, 16, 39, 55, 56, 68, 77, 82, 90; *see also* Slogans

panic, 47
patience, 80
peace, 21
peer pressure, 63

perfect, 50, 62
perfection, 2, 5
power, 2, 3, 4, 5, 6, 7, 8, 10, 11, 13, 14, 17, 18, 19, 20, 21, 22, 23, 28, 30, 32, 34, 35, 36, 37, 38, 40, 41, 42, 44, 47, 48, 51, 53, 54, 57, 58, 59, 63, 65, 67, 68, 71, 72, 73, 75, 82, 84, 87, 90
powerless, 4, 5, 9, 10, 12, 16, 18, 24, 29, 35, 38, 40, 41, 42, 84, 90
pray, 2, 14, 27, 37, 46, 68, 75, 82, 90
prayer, 1, 3, 7, 17, 21, 32, 33, 38, 70
praying, 6
procrastination, 25
program, the, 3, 19, 44, 49, 61, 78, 80, 86, 89
progress, 2, 5, 49
Progress, Not Perfection, 2; *see also* Slogans
Promises, the, 26, 48
A Puff Away From a Pack a Day, 10; *see also* Slogans

quality, 2
quit, 5, 6, 7, 8, 9, 12, 13, 14, 16, 17, 23, 25, 26, 27, 28, 29, 30, 38, 39, 40, 43, 50, 51, 55, 56, 59, 66, 73, 79, 81, 83, 88, 89
quitting, 7, 9, 12, 17, 34, 52, 89

recovery, 2, 4, 7, 12, 13, 21, 28,

32, 45, 49, 54, 62, 63, 64, 66, 72, 75, 79, 80, 81, 84
relapse, 21, 88
relationships, 90
relax, 1, 5, 15, 18, 66
release, 38
rewards, 51, 62

sanity, 19, 37
secrets, 38, 49
self-esteem, 15, 21, 63, 82
self-pity, 1
self-respect, 74
self-will, 20
self-worth, 3
senses, 74
serenity, 24, 25, 32, 33, 50
service, 55, 80, 90
shame, 46
sharing, 56
slipping, 23
slogans, 3, 15
   Easy Does It, 15
   Experience, Strength and Hope, 17, 20, 56, 84, 86
   Happy, Joyous and Free, 12, 27, 42, 75
   Keep Coming Back, 30, 61, 86, 87, 88, 95
   Keep It Simple, 39, 95
   Let Go and Let God, 5, 18, 36, 57
   Life on Life's Terms, 32, 67
   One Day At a Time, 6, 7, 11, 16, 39, 55, 56, 68, 77, 82, 90
   Progress, Not Perfection, 2
   A Puff Away From a Pack a Day, 10
   Walk the Walk, 35
smoking, 3
spiritual, 20, 42, 53, 72, 75, 82, 85
spiritual awakening, 85
spirituality, 72
sponsor, 5, 13, 19, 24, 27, 62
sponsorship, 3
staying quit, 56
Step One, 4, 9, 12
Step Two, 37
Step Three, 33, 40
Step Four, 38, 48, 49
Step Five, 49
Step Eight, 24
Step Nine, 24
Step Ten, 62
Step Eleven, 70
Step Twelve, 85
Steps, the, 34, 38, 69, 84
strength, 17, 20, 22, 28, 56, 79, 84, 86, 87
stress, 15, 22, 55, 66, 71
stuff (verb), 45
support, 2, 11, 12, 17, 44, 54, 63, 81, 87, 89
surrender, 4, 17, 24, 25, 27, 28, 30, 35, 36, 43, 70

time, 3
tools, 3, 21, 49, 72, 90
Tradition Three, 30

Traditions, the, 42
triggers, 4
trust, 30, 54, 67, 68, 73
truth, 4, 8, 14, 49, 50, 57, 73, 75, 79
turned it over, 29
Twelve Steps, 7, 31, 38, 41, 42, 48, 49, 72, 75, 81, 82

unconditional love, 54
"Using," 2

Walk the Walk, 35; see also Slogans
weight, 29
welcome, 42
will, 1, 19, 35, 36
willing, 16, 20, 30, 35, 55, 84, 88
willingness, 6, 51, 75
willpower, 16, 19, 20, 35
wisdom, 18, 19, 70, 84
working the steps, 34